The Quilt of Belonging

Stitching Together the Stories of a Nation

Janice Weaver

MAPLE
TREE
PRESS

Maple Tree Press Inc.
51 Front Street East, Suite 200, Toronto, Ontario M5E 1B3
www.mapletreepress.com

Distributed in Canada by Raincoast Books
9050 Shaughnessy Street, Vancouver, British Columbia V6P 6E5

Distributed in the United States by Publishers Group West
1700 Fourth Street, Berkeley, California 94710

Cataloguing in Publication Data

Weaver, Janice
The quilt of belonging : stitching together the stories of a nation / Janice Weaver.

Includes index.
ISBN 13: 978-1-897066-49-2 (bound) / ISBN 10: 1-897066-49-X (bound)
ISBN 13: 978-1-897066-50-8 (pbk.) / ISBN 10: 1-897066-50-3 (pbk.)

   1. Quilts — Canada. 2. Invitation, the Quilt of Belonging (Organization).
   3. Immigrants — Canada. I. Title.

NK9113.A1W42 2006   746.46'0971   C2005-904643-0

Design: Blair Kerrigan/Glyphics
Photography: Ken McLaren

We acknowledge the financial support of the Canada Council for the Arts, the Ontario Arts Council,
the Government of Canada through the Book Publishing Industry Development Program (BPIDP),
and the Government of Ontario through the Ontario Media Development Corporation's Book
Initiative for our publishing activities.

ONTARIO ARTS COUNCIL
CONSEIL DES ARTS DE L'ONTARIO

Printed in China

A   B   C   D   E   F

Contents

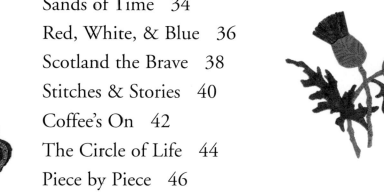

Creating the Quilt

Even before there was a nation called Canada, people were coming to this land to take advantage of all it had to offer — oceans teeming with fish, prairie fields overrun with buffalo, vast acres of fertile soil, the chance for a better life. Later, they came to escape war, hunger, and disease; to help build our railways; and to clear our land and plant our crops. They came to be teachers, nurses, students, and storekeepers, and they still come every day, hoping to start over in a place that offers freedom and opportunity.

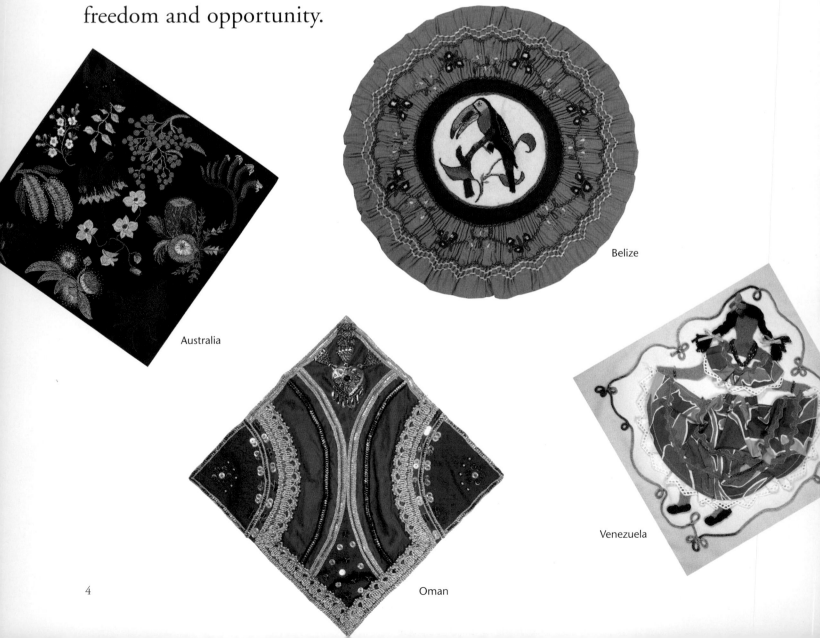

Gambia

Australia

Belize

Oman

Venezuela

Burma

Esther Bryan, a visual artist, had always believed that Canada was a richer country for what those people brought — and continue to bring — to it. When she made a trip to Slovakia, her father's homeland, that belief only grew stronger. She saw people there living a different, much harder kind of life, and she began thinking more about the world and her place in it. She realized that although each of us experiences life in our own unique way, we also have so much in common. "I learned that everyone needs to feel accepted," she recalls, "no matter who they are or where they live." She became convinced that every single person on this earth — regardless of their age, their abilities, or the circumstances of their life — has something of value to offer, a contribution to make.

When she got back to Canada, Esther began thinking about ways to honour the contributions of all Canadians, old and new. "I wanted to create something that would celebrate the whole fabric that is Canada," she says. "I wanted to show the path from separateness to wholeness to belonging." She decided to make a massive quilt, a monument in stitches and fabric to the patchwork of people who have come to Canada from many places and helped build this country. The quilt would include a block for every nation of the world and for each of Canada's major aboriginal groups. And every one of those blocks would be prepared by a Canadian with a connection to that nation or group.

Luxembourg

Carrier

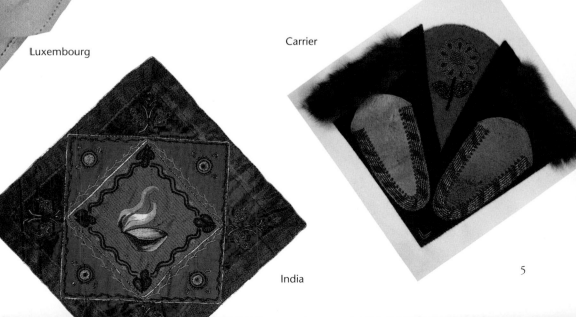

India

5

To get started, a volunteer researcher, Daphne Howells, began sifting through immigration records. She soon learned that as of the first day of the new millennium — January 1, 2000 — there was at least one person from every country on earth living in Canada. But tracking down representatives from each of those countries was an immense challenge that involved countless letters, phone calls, e-mails, and visits to community and church groups, immigration centres, and embassies. It took close to six years — almost as long as was needed to make the quilt itself — to find all those people and make them part of the project.

Those who didn't have the skill to make the blocks themselves instead contributed their ideas, designs, and materials to the quilt's army of volunteer textile artists. Some passed on fabrics they'd carried across the ocean when they first came to Canada. Others donated precious silks and linens that had been in their family for generations. Still others offered materials of a different sort, from moosehide to porcupine quills to butterfly wings.

Slowly, the Quilt of Belonging began to take shape. The volunteers had blocks from some of the world's greatest

nations and its most remote spots — from Russia and China to Tuvalu and Bhutan — and from many of Canada's major aboriginal groups. As they submitted their work, the participants were invited to choose a coloured fabric to border their blocks. In effect, they were being asked to find their own place within the quilt, for these borders — not geography, politics, or religion — determined how the blocks were ultimately arranged.

In the end, the Quilt of Belonging has become a powerful symbol of Canada itself. All the blocks are separate and distinct, like the people who created them and the nations they represent. But each one is also connected to its neighbours by a continuous length of cording, a colourful strand of thread that links the blocks just as we are linked to our fellow citizens by our obligations and responsibilities as Canadians. "The quilt is a vision of what we can and should be," Esther says. "There can be a place for everyone in Canada, just as there is a place for everyone in the Quilt of Belonging."

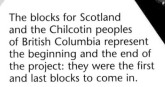

The blocks for Scotland and the Chilcotin peoples of British Columbia represent the beginning and the end of the project: they were the first and last blocks to come in.

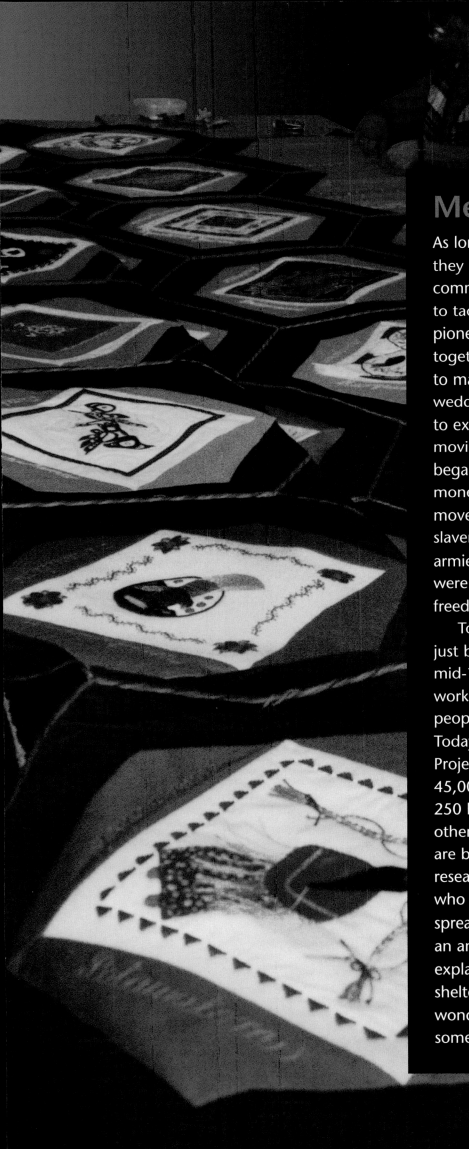

Memories & Messages

As long as people have been making quilts, they have been using them to tell stories, to commemorate important events, and even to tackle social and political issues. Early pioneer women in North America pieced together leftover fabric into memory quilts to mark special family occasions, such as weddings or births, or into friendship quilts to exchange with loved ones who were moving far away. Later, American women began making and selling quilts to raise money for causes like the abolition movement (which worked towards ending slavery) and to buy supplies for Civil War armies. There is even evidence that quilts were used to tell runaway slaves the route to freedom along the Underground Railroad.

To this day, quilts are used as more than just bedcoverings or wall hangings. In the mid-1980s, a small group of people began working on a massive quilt to honour people whose lives had been lost to AIDS. Today, that quilt — known as the NAMES Project — has grown to include about 45,000 panels and is the size of more than 250 basketball courts. And it has inspired other projects along the same lines. Quilts are being used to raise money for cancer research, to increase awareness of children who are neglected and abused, and to spread peace around the world. "Quilts are an amazing medium to work in," Esther explains, "because they express comfort and shelter, as well as beauty. Quilting is a wonderfully uplifting metaphor for making something whole out of many pieces."

The Quilt of Belonging: At a Glance

Total number of squares: 263

Number of squares representing Canada's First Peoples: 70

Number of volunteers involved with project: Into the thousands

Length of project, from concept to finished quilt: 6 years

Unusual materials used: Guatemalan worry dolls, cowrie shells, porcupine quills, clock hands, moccasins, postage stamps, sealskin, abalone shell buttons, Scottish tartans, miniature paddles

Size of each individual block:
28 by 28 centimetres (11 by 11 inches), or
40 by 45 centimetres (16 by 18 inches) with the border

Size of finished quilt:
36 metres (120 feet) long and 3.5 metres (10 feet) high

3.5 metres (10 feet) high

36 metres (120 feet) long

The Blocks

War & Peace

A patchwork dove, a symbol of peace, swoops and soars high above a fanciful village scene in the block for El Salvador, a country that is struggling to rebuild itself after a devastating civil war. Beneath the dove's outstretched wings sits an umbrella-like guanacaste tree, which represents stability and growth, and offers some much-needed protection from the blazing red sun above. On the village outskirts, several white-washed, red-roofed houses jockey for room by the shore of some brilliant blue water.

The block-makers used traditional Salvadoran wool thread and a white woven cloth backdrop to create their bright and cheerful Central American landscape. The embroidered block has a simple, child-like feel that reflects the Native Indian ancestry of most Salvadorans. Its vibrant colours and shining sun suggest hope for the future, while the symbolism of the dove is hard to miss for a country that has been so scarred by war.

Comes a Horseman

A lone horseman gallops across the steppe (a grassy plain), his bright blue *khurim* jacket flapping in the wind, in this block representing Mongolia. He is a traditional nomadic herder, a man who moves from place to place with his animals. In the background sits his yurt, a round, felt tent that has provided generations of herders just like him with protection from the sweltering hot days and crisp, cool nights of Mongolia's mostly desert landscape.

The people of this remote central Asian country are mainly Mongols descended from the thirteenth-century conqueror Genghis Khan and his warriors. They're very proud of their long, colourful history, their tribal loyalties, and their centuries-old nomadic culture. In this block, that nomadic way of life is represented by the ram's horn border that encircles our sheep-herding horseman. The ram's horn pattern — cut into the red fabric and repeated in the white — also symbolizes prosperity, for in a country where land was historically shared by everyone in the tribe, it was the size of a man's herd that determined his wealth.

A Stitch in Time

The block-makers used almost every imaginable technique — from lace- and leatherwork to cross-stitching, needlepoint, and weaving — to create the 263 squares that make up the Quilt of Belonging.

Many of the most striking blocks were appliquéd, a method that involves cutting out pieces of cloth and sewing them to a background to create a pattern or picture. The block for Namibia, a nation on the southwestern coast of Africa, is a good example. The square features a San hunter — sometimes called a Bushman — whose arms, legs, head, and body have all been cut out of bright red cotton. In his right hand he holds a crooked walking stick, and a loincloth made from fish bones hangs about his waist. Even the rusty sands of the Namib Desert have been created out of orange-coloured fabric and layered against a pale blue cotton sky.

The block for Namibia's neighbour, Botswana, looks completely different. It was made using batik, where designs and pictures are created on cloth by waxing areas not meant to be coloured and dipping the whole fabric in dye. In this block, the chief's elaborate ceremonial chair sits amid round village huts. Several blue puddles — evidence of a rare and recent rainstorm — lie nearby, waiting for the hot sun of the Kalahari Desert to make them disappear.

Botswana

Namibia

Denmark

The Danish block-makers used embroidery to create their quaint Scandinavian village scene. Tiny thatched-roof houses huddle near the shore of a bright blue lake, and a stork, a symbol of good luck, perches on one chimney. A bicycle, a favourite way for Danes to travel across their country's low, mostly flat landscape, leans against the wall of one of the houses, while in the background the Danish flag flaps gently in the breeze. The whole scene is encircled with a Christmas-inspired border of black cats, tiny evergreens, red-hatted elves, and piping-hot bowls of sweet rice pudding.

Intricate beadwork brings to life the block for the Plains Cree, who live on the prairie grasslands of Alberta and Saskatchewan. The block-maker used hundreds of different coloured beads to create a collage of images, including a rainbow, a starburst, and an eagle's head and feather. Like the medicine wheel on pages 44–45, this block is built around the four aboriginal colours of man — black, white, red, and yellow. Here, they represent the four points on the compass, signifying the close relationship especially, the four stages of life and, between people and nature.

Plains Cree

Animal Kingdom

Several brightly coloured cotton animals are appliquéd onto a panel of black fabric in the block for Benin, a western African nation with a long and sometimes tragic history. Appliqué-work — along with weaving, woodcarving, goldwork, and similar crafts — is one of the country's centuries-old "royal arts." Long-ago artisans laboured away in the service of Benin's kings, creating cloth banners, jewellery, and statuettes that told of the rulers' triumphs in war and popularity among their people.

In a country where most people cannot read or write, crafts still have an important role to play in passing stories on from generation to generation. Modern-day appliqué-makers continue to create wall hangings and tapestries that show the great feats of Benin's twelve ancient kings. In this block, the appliquéd animals stand for three of the most influential of those rulers. Gangnihessou, the first leader of Benin's historic kingdom and a man whose voice, according to legend, could never be silenced, is represented by the bright red bird that seems to be getting ready to sing. The mighty lion caught mid-roar is for Glele, the king who helped the nation reach the height of its power. And the plunging shark is for the last ruler, Behanzin, who fought fiercely (but without success) against the soldiers who were trying to take over his kingdom and turn it into a colony of France.

Under the

Dragon's Tail

The centrepiece is a friendly dragon with its toes splayed out. Dragons are a powerful symbol of good luck and prosperity to the Chinese, who believe these mythical creatures shelter them from evil, bring rain for their crops, and promote health, wealth, and wisdom.

The dragon is surrounded by four pink lotus flowers. These delicate plants, which emerge from the mud in swampy waters, represent purity and perseverance, and are sacred to the people of China. Because they have a stem that's easy to bend but hard to break, they also signify the bond between two people in love.

Four graceful butterflies, their wings outlined in fine gold thread, flutter in the corners of the block. Butterflies are able to transform themselves from wormlike caterpillars into the most beautiful of all insects, and so they represent change. They're an especially strong symbol to Chinese Canadians, who have been coming to Canada for about 150 years in search of a better life.

The background is made of deep black silk, the strongest of all natural fibres. The Chinese were the first people to learn to make silk, and for hundreds and hundreds of years, they jealously guarded the secret of its origins. To this day, China still produces more silk than any other country in the world.

True Colours

The block for the Solomon Islands is a riot of colours and shapes. In rich reds, deep browns, brilliant blues, and earthy yellows and oranges, it tells the story of life in this archipelago (chain of islands) northeast of Australia.

The figures in the top half of the block represent the nation's three indigenous peoples: the Melanesians, Polynesians, and Micronesians. They seem to be stretching their long arms to the bright blue tropical sky and the hot sun overhead. Beneath their feet, four frigate birds — their slender wings and streamlined bodies stitched in white — plunge headfirst into the warm waters of the South Pacific. These lucky frigates have beaten the islands' fishermen to the five blue tuna darting about underneath the waves.

This unique block recreates a painting by a British Columbia artist who came to Canada from the Solomon Islands to study. His vibrant artwork — full of strong, bold lines; bright colours; and geometric shapes like circles and triangles — has the feel of island wood carvings, a craft practised by his ancestors for centuries.

Our Founding Nations

Every major First Nations, Métis, and Inuit group in Canada is represented in the quilt. Their seventy blocks make up the foundation row and wrap the quilt on its two sides, a sign of respect for our founding nations.

The block for the Eastern Cree of northern Quebec uses white-tanned moosehide to create the snowy backdrop for a mythical star-chasing bear. The bear's shoulders are loaded down with coloured beads — once used as currency by North American Natives — which he tosses in the air to fill the soft blue night sky with stars.

The Hare block features an Arctic rose, one of the few flowering plants that can survive the cold of the tribe's native Northwest Territories. It's a powerful symbol of the determination and perseverance of these people, as well as a reminder of the delicate beauty of the North.

Hare

Eastern Cree

A Delta braid is the centrepiece of the Gwich'in block. The women of this Yukon tribe make these braids by stitching together many layers of fabric to create bright and bold geometric patterns. Here, it's almost as if the braid — with its fifty-five separate layers overlapping and weaving together — represents the Gwich'in people themselves as they look back to their ancestors and forward to generations yet to be born.

The quilt even includes a block for Newfoundland's tragic Beothuk people, who all fell victim to starvation and diseases brought by European settlers. The block shows a map of their ancient settlement at Boyd's Cove, now a modern-day archeological site. It also includes a drawing of a dancing woman, based on a sketch made by Shawnadithit, the last of the Beothuk. Created with bark, fur,

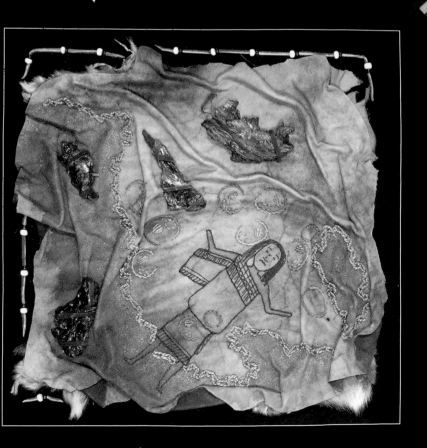

Gwich'in

Beothuk

First Light

Two Native Indian women sit together at the centre of the block for Ecuador, a small country on the west coast of South America. Each one wears a handmade Panama hat and carries a warm shawl known as a *chalina*. It looks as if they've just put down their water jugs to watch the sun climb from behind Mount Chimborazo, the country's highest peak. The friendly scene is encircled with colourful woven bands in typical Ecuadorean patterns.

Native customs are still very much alive in Ecuador. Most citizens are Indians descended from the ancient Incas. Many still live in isolated regions; speak Quechua, a Native language; and survive by selling handmade pottery and traditional cloths like those in the quilt square. This block uses all the colours and textures of South America — from the tightly woven wool bands to the blues and pinks and greens of the women's clothes — to create a striking portrait of daily life in Ecuador.

Where Palm

A graceful palm tree dominates the block for Nigeria, a country on the western coast of Africa. The tree's oversize leaves shelter two beaded clusters of date palm fruits, which Nigerians harvest to make medicines and palm oil for cooking. In the background, a ribbon of hand-woven and hand-dyed silk creates the rippling waters of the mighty Niger River, a time-honoured means of getting Nigerians from place to place and an important source of hydroelectric power for the country.

Palm trees also grace the block for Mauritius, an island in the Indian Ocean, east of Africa. In this piece, three trees seem to sway gently in the breeze while the bright blue waters of the island's Black River glide slowly past. The palm trees add to the scene's tropical feel, but the focus is on a dodo, the famous flightless bird that European sailors hunted to extinction on the island in the 1600s. This imagined survivor sits in her nest protecting her single egg, perhaps a symbol of the fragile future of this volcanic island itself.

Nigeria

Trees Sway

Mauritius

Rising Sun

A beautiful woman in traditional dress, her face powdered white in a centuries-old display of beauty, gazes out from the block for Japan. Her hand gently supports a piece of fine parchment, while over her shoulder the name of the block-maker has been drawn in elegant Japanese characters. The quiet scene is enclosed by a double band of gold braiding and finished with a thin thread of Japanese gold work.

This block is an example of an ancient Japanese art form called *oshie*. The block-maker cut all the individual sections out of rich silk, padded them with cotton, then placed them on a sea of soft white and pink clouds like the pieces of a jigsaw puzzle. The end result is a textured portrait that seems to lift right off its fabric backing. Even the woman's lustrous black hair was created from strips of silk and painstakingly arranged on her head strand by individual strand.

Island-hopping

Many of the blocks for the world's island nations use the same family of colours — bright yellows, soft greens, watery blues, and fiery reds. They bring to mind the warm sand, ocean waves, and brilliant tropical sunsets shared by all these places, even when they're found in opposite corners of the globe.

St. Vincent and the Grenadines

In the block for the West Indian islands of St. Vincent and the Grenadines, an enormous sequinned breadfruit, a tropical plant with pulp that tastes like freshly baked bread, takes centre stage. The square uses yellow, green, and blue — the colours of the islands' flag — to evoke the sun-bleached Caribbean landscape.

The national flag also inspired the quilt square for Seychelles, an archipelago of about ninety islands off the southeast coast of Africa. Five bold blocks of colour — the same colours that are found in the stripes on the flag — host scenes of daily island life. In the yellow section, the hot African sun rises behind the Morne Seychellois, the islands' highest peak. Next to that, an old-

Seychelles

fashioned sailing vessel — like the ones that first brought settlers to Seychelles in the 1700s — skims along some gentle ocean waves. Below, two Seychellois dance in the tropical heat, while in the last two sections, a pair of giant coco-de-mer trees drop their fruit, an unusual double coconut that grows nowhere else in the world.

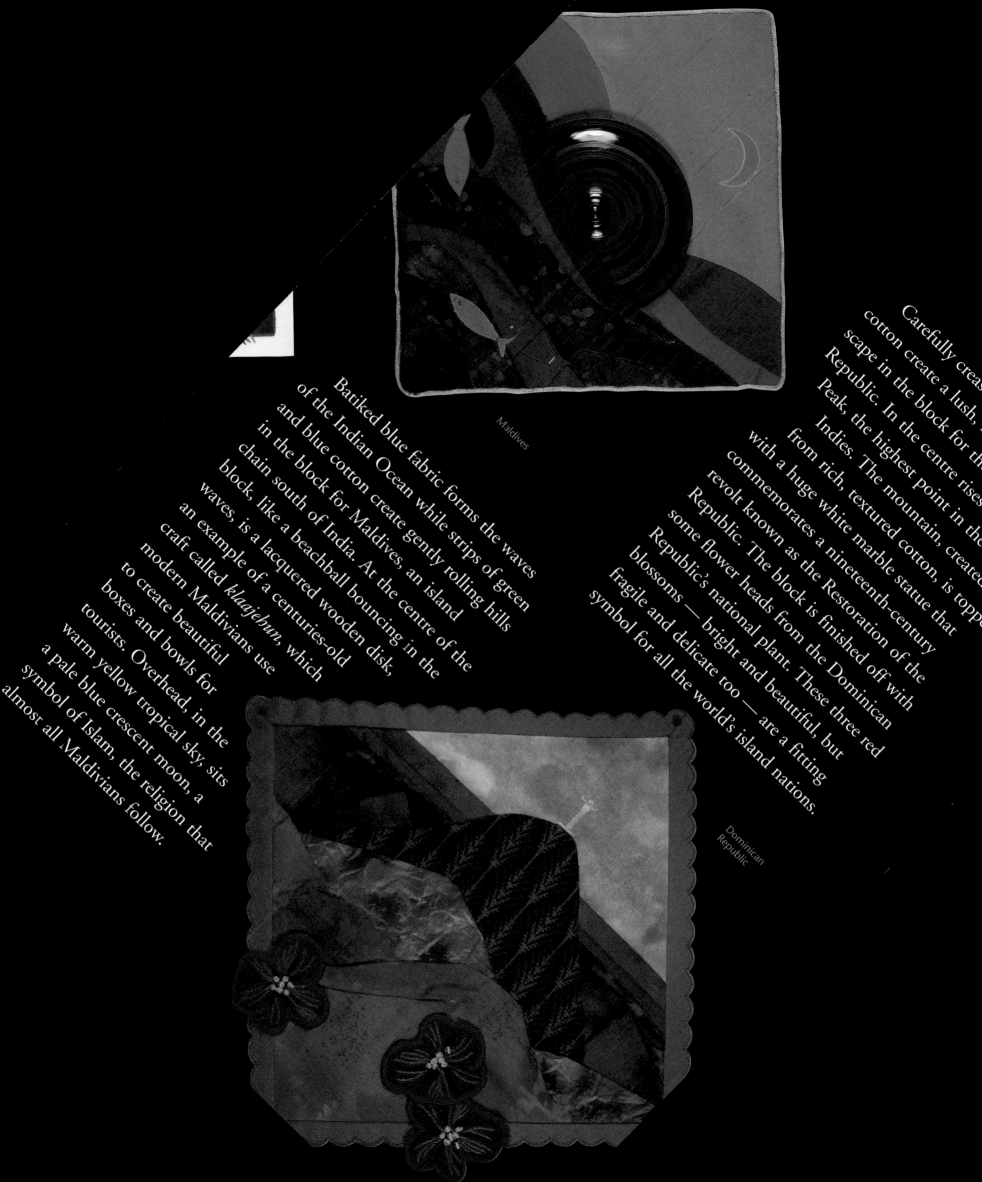

Carefully crea[...] cotton create a lush, [...] scape in the block for th[...] Republic. In the centre rises [...] Peak, the highest point in the [...] Indies. The mountain, created [...] from rich, textured cotton, is topp[...] with a huge white marble statue that commemorates a nineteenth-century revolt known as the Restoration of the Republic. The block is finished off with some flower heads from the Dominican Republic's national plant. These three red blossoms — bright and beautiful, but fragile and delicate too — are a fitting symbol for all the world's island nations.

Maldives

Batiked blue fabric forms the waves of the Indian Ocean while strips of green and blue cotton create gently rolling hills in the block for Maldives, an island chain south of India. At the centre of the block, like a beachball bouncing in the waves, is a lacquered wooden disk, an example of a centuries-old craft called *kuajehun*, which modern Maldivians use to create beautiful boxes and bowls for tourists. Overhead, in the warm yellow tropical sky, sits a pale blue crescent moon, a symbol of Islam, the religion that almost all Maldivians follow.

Dominican Republic

Sands of Time

The soft, warm colours of the Egyptian block remind us of the country's desert landscape. Made from bright strips of local cotton and encircled with a border inspired by the archways often found on mosques (Islamic houses of worship), the block shows a lonely camel trudging across the hot desert sand. The Pyramids of Giza, one of the Seven Wonders of the Ancient World and the last resting place of three of Egypt's greatest kings, rise up in the background. In the surrounding border sit four lotus blossoms, much like the ones that are also found on the block for China. These plants, which grow along the banks of the Nile, are a symbol of one of Egypt's first kingdoms and an important part of many of this ancient country's creation stories.

This block is another example of appliqué, which in Egypt is a craft usually practised by men. Once used to decorate the inside walls of the tents of desert nomads, appliqué is today most often found on everyday items like pillowcases and bedspreads. Here, the appliquéd square brings together the gentle turquoise of the Nile River, the rich browns and golds of the Saharan sands, and the bright white of the blazing North African sun.

Red, White,

The block for the United States is rich in symbolism. Using both needlework and traditional quilting — fabric arts that have been practised in the U.S. since the earliest days of European settlement — the piece calls to mind pioneer life, the principles of freedom and opportunity, and even the American flag.

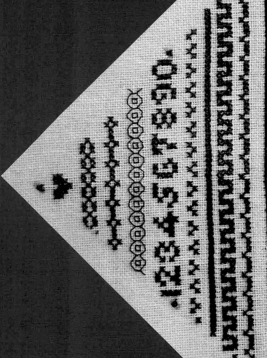

The block is all done in red, white, and blue — the official colours of the United States. Red stands for courage, white for innocence, and blue for justice.

& Blue

E pluribus unum is the Latin motto of the United States. The words mean "Out of many, one," and they refer to the creation of one nation out of the thirteen original colonies. To many people, they also stand for the millions of immigrants who have come to America and helped make it the great and powerful nation it is today.

Made using a traditional log cabin design, the four central squares signify the rustic homes of the earliest American pioneers. The solid red squares at their centres represent the hearth, or fireplace, the symbolic heart of any home. The pattern is dark on one side and light on the other, like the sunny and shady sides of a house.

Several red, white, and blue threads are loosely tied at the block's centre. Busy pioneer women often secured the layers of their quilts together with special knots, instead of using quilting techniques that took more time and effort than they could spare.

The borders are done in a sampler pattern. In colonial America, mothers taught their young daughters to make samplers so they could practise their needlework while they learned their numbers and letters.

Scotland the Brave

Like a patchwork quilt, the block for Scotland was made from pieces of leftover cloth. Twenty-eight tiny squares cut from a variety of tartan fabrics — representing some of the clans and regions of Scotland — are arranged around the block's edges like the thick stone walls of a Highland castle.

At the heart of the block, in the middle of what would be the castle's courtyard, two thistles sit nestled in a stand of heather. Both plants blanket the hills and valleys of the Scottish Highlands like freshly fallen snow. The heather, like a four-leaf clover, is believed to bring good luck to anyone who picks it, while the thistle is a symbol of protection. As Scotland's national emblem, this prickly plant carries the motto "No one harms me without punishment." Here, the thistles — which seem to be bending their soft purple heads in the breeze — represent the resilience of the Scottish people, as well as their fighting spirit.

Coffee's On

You can almost smell the coffee brewing in the block for the United Arab Emirates, a federation of states on the Arabian Peninsula. Its centrepiece is a stitched golden *dallah*, a coffee pot that represents the warmth and hospitality of the Arab people. The *dallah* is framed by a border of hand-woven woollen fabrics in green, red, and black, the colours of the Bedouin, the desert nomads of the Arab world.

A tiny coffee pot — this one hand-crafted in solid brass — is also the most important element of the block for Syria, an Arab nation on the Mediterranean Sea. Set against a background of antique silk damask (a fabric that takes its name from Syria's capital city, Damascus), this coffee pot is called a *cezve*. It's surrounded by two sheaves of wheat, a plant that was probably first cultivated (grown as a source of food) in Syria as much as eleven thousand years ago, and some olive branches, an ancient symbol of peace. The entire block is encircled with a richly embroidered band of green that's cut in a scalloped pattern much like the border of the Egyptian block.

Syria

United Arab Emirates

The Circle of

The quilt includes a special square that represents all Canada's First Peoples — Natives, Métis, and Inuit — as a group. This bold geometric block is a traditional medicine wheel, an ancient symbol for the circle of life. It's divided into sections of four, a number that is sacred to most aboriginal peoples.

The wheel expresses four key personality traits. White stands for wisdom, yellow for purity, red for love, and black for creativity.

Life

The wheel's sections stand for the four points on the compass, the four stages of life (birth, childhood, adulthood, and old age), the four seasons, and the four elements (earth, air, fire, and water). Here, the snowy white segment symbolizes winter and the north.

The sections also represent the idea of the four races of humankind: whites, Asians, aboriginal peoples, and blacks. In this way, the wheel offers a subtle message about the need for all the world's people to respect one another's differences and live peacefully together.

The whole circle is surrounded by a field of green, representing both the earth and the spirit world. The wheel reminds us of the importance of balancing all the aspects of our lives — emotional, spiritual, intellectual, and physical — and learning to exist in harmony with the world around us.

Piece by Piece

Rising in the background of the block for the Caribbean nation of St. Lucia are the Pitons, two ancient volcanic cones that dominate the island's landscape. The peaks, created out of rich green linen, are silhouetted against a swatch of bright orange-yellow fabric, so like the sun-bleached West Indian sky.

In the foreground, perched in the crook of a gnarled tree, sits a Jacquot, an endangered parrot that's native to St. Lucia. This beautiful bird, embroidered in satin threads, brings together all the colours of island life — the soft blues of the saltwater sea, the deep browns and emerald greens of the fertile soil and lush vegetation, and the fiery reds of tropical sunsets.

The whole scene is enclosed within a heart-shaped border of lightweight madras cotton and delicate eyelet lace, both taken from St. Lucia's national dress. The block is topped with a miniature headdress called a *tête en l'air* (head in the sky). Island women tie these brightly coloured scarves in different ways to represent their romantic status. One peak means the wearer is single and available; two peaks mean she is involved but could be convinced to stray; and three (as here) mean she is committed to another.

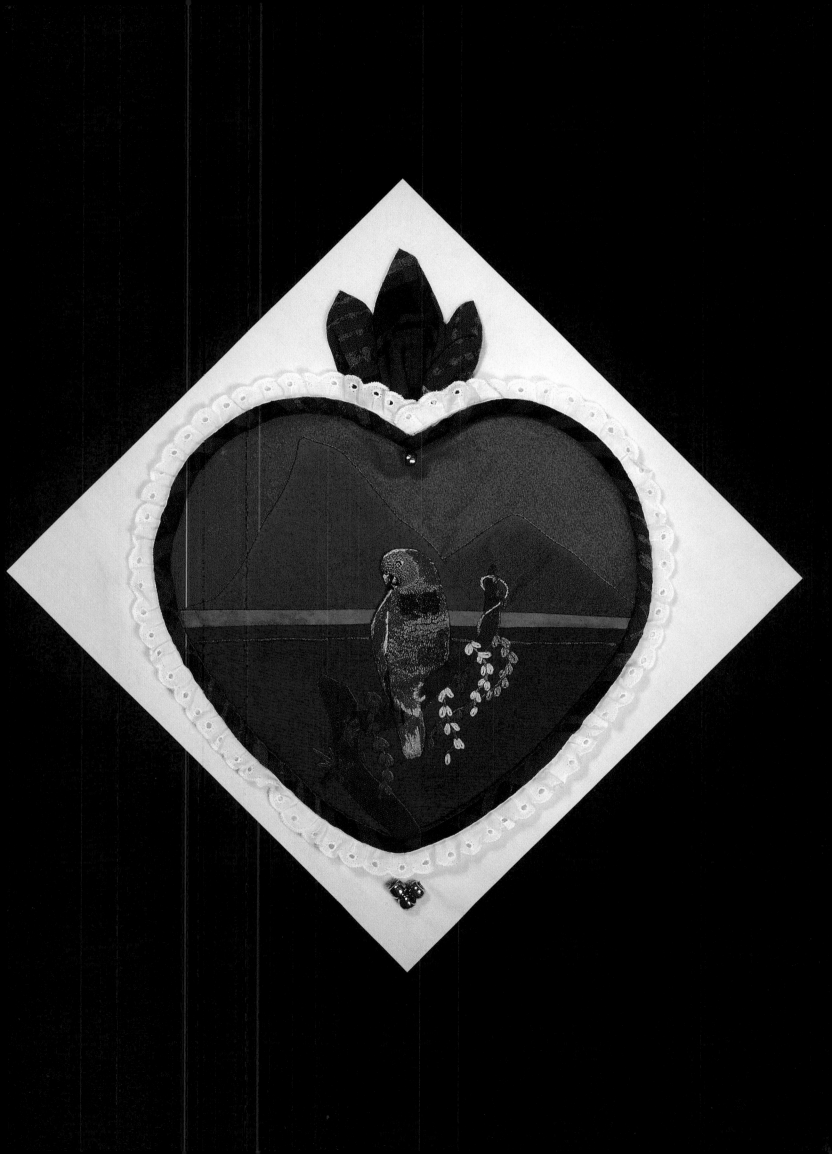

Not all the block-makers used fabrics to create their quilt pieces. Some turned to unexpected materials — like beads and porcupine quills and even postage stamps — to make their blocks come to life.

The block for the Inuvialuit people of Canada's western Arctic was crafted from real sealskin and stitched with sinew (thread made from animal tissue). The piece features an Inuk man performing the Alaskan High Kick. With one hand tightly grasping his floor and the other tightly grasping his left foot, the man kicks up at a stuffed sealskin ball in a traditional northern display of agility and athletic skill.

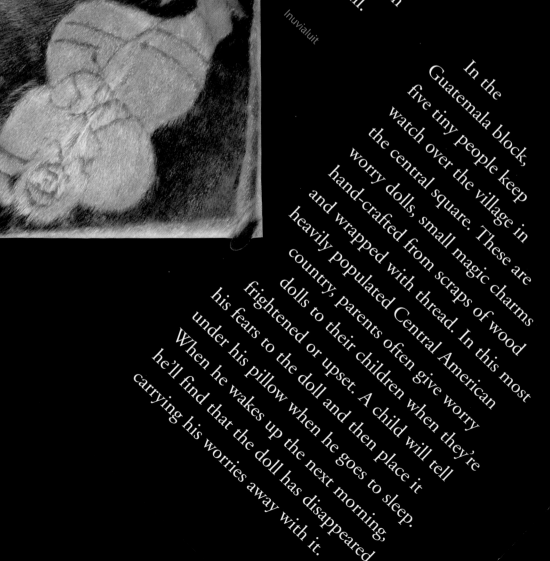

Inuvialuit

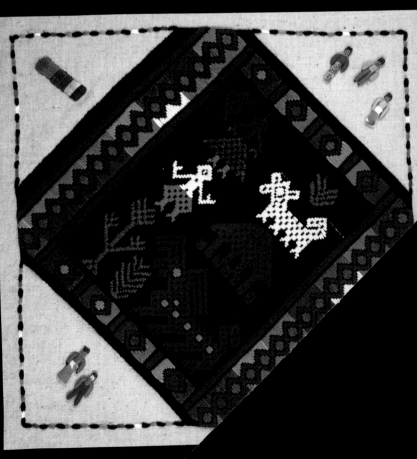

Guatemala

In the Guatemala block, five tiny people keep watch over the village in the central square. These are worry dolls, small magic charms hand-crafted from scraps of wood and wrapped with thread. In this most heavily populated Central American country, parents often give worry dolls to their children when they're frightened or upset. A child will tell his fears to the doll and then place it under his pillow when he goes to sleep. When he wakes up the next morning, he'll find that the doll has disappeared, carrying his worries away with it.

The block for the Central African Republic looks as if it could float away much like the fears of those Guatemalan children. Made from butterfly wings that children and local craftspeople harvest from the forest floor, the block shows two women pounding spices in a time-worn mortar. The wings of the butterflies can clearly be seen in the sleeves of their shirts, the folds of their skirts, and the bright, almost shimmering green hats on their heads.

The block for Tonga, a kingdom of islands in the South Pacific, was created from *tapa* cloth. This papery thin cloth, which island women make by pounding the bark of the mulberry tree until it's flat, is most often used to commemorate important events, like weddings or funerals. In this block, the *tapa* has been stencilled with a geometric flower and framed by a cross-hatched border that calls to mind the tightly woven fibres of the cloth itself.

Central African Republic

Tonga

A Helping Hand

In the block for Bangladesh, an Asian nation bordered by India, two beautiful women pound grain with a mortar and pestle, just as their ancestors have done for centuries. The women are dressed in colourful saris to protect them from the heat of the blazing sun above, and they work together to make their labour go faster. Although Bangladesh is one of the most densely populated nations on the globe, most of its citizens still live in the countryside and work the land with simple tools like these women are doing.

This block was crafted by a well-known Bangladeshi embroidery artist who came to Canada in 1998. She has used many special embroidery techniques to create this beautiful village scene, from the widely spaced stitches of the earth and sky to the tightly packed French knots that make up the thatched roof of the simple bamboo hut in the background.

Flower

A special block was created for the United Kingdom and its overseas territories, which include islands in the South Pacific, the Indian Ocean, the Caribbean Sea, and even the Antarctic. The block-makers decided to use national flowers to represent each territory.

At the corners of the block, marking the points of a compass, are four plants that represent the United Kingdom itself. They are the rose for England (in the north position), the thistle for Scotland (east), the shamrock for Northern Ireland (south), and the daffodil for Wales (west).

Arranging

For the ice-covered British Antarctic Territory, which has almost no plant life except for some mosses and algae, the block-makers stitched one tiny, perfect snowflake.

The remote Pitcairn Islands, settled in the 1700s by the mutineers from the British ship *Bounty*, had no national flower, so one had to be chosen specially for the quilt. The islanders selected a bloom called the high white, which has since been honoured with its own Pitcairn Island postage stamp as well.

All the flowers are surrounded by a leafy vine that both separates and connects them. The vine, used often in English embroidery, is a powerful symbol for the territories themselves, which are scattered throughout the world but still linked together in the Commonwealth of Nations.

At the centre of the block sits a gold-and-purple crown, a symbol of the British monarchy. The United Kingdom Overseas Territories are ruled as though they are part of the United Kingdom, and all recognize the British monarch as the head of government.

From Far & Wide

In the block for Canada, hundreds of tiny glass
beads form an image that reminds us of the
outline left by a maple leaf on a wet city sidewalk.
Set against a velvet background the colour of
Canada's flag, the beads cluster together in
groups, just as Canadians themselves mass along the country's vast
border with the United States. The leaf those beads create — its eleven
points representing each of Canada's ten provinces and its northern
territories — is sometimes clear and distinct and sometimes harder to make
out. It suggests wide-open spaces, freedom, and a story that is still unfolding.

Visitors to the quilt have to look closely to appreciate the subtle beauty of
this simple maple leaf. Like most Canadians, it is understated and modest; it
doesn't shout for our attention. At times, it's more clearly defined by what's
outside of it than it is by the beads themselves — just as Canadians
sometimes need to be reminded by others of what they and their country
have to offer the world.

Make Your Own Square

Are you feeling inspired by the beautiful quilt pieces in this book? Then maybe now is the time to try your hand at making one of your own. Don't despair, though, if you know you can't create something as elaborate as the padded, three-dimensional Japanese block on pages 30–31. While it's true that many of the squares in the Quilt of Belonging were made using complicated needlework or crafts like weaving and batik, some were put together with simple stitches by volunteers who had never done much sewing before. If you find the right materials and settle on a good theme, you can make a block that looks great with just a few basic skills.

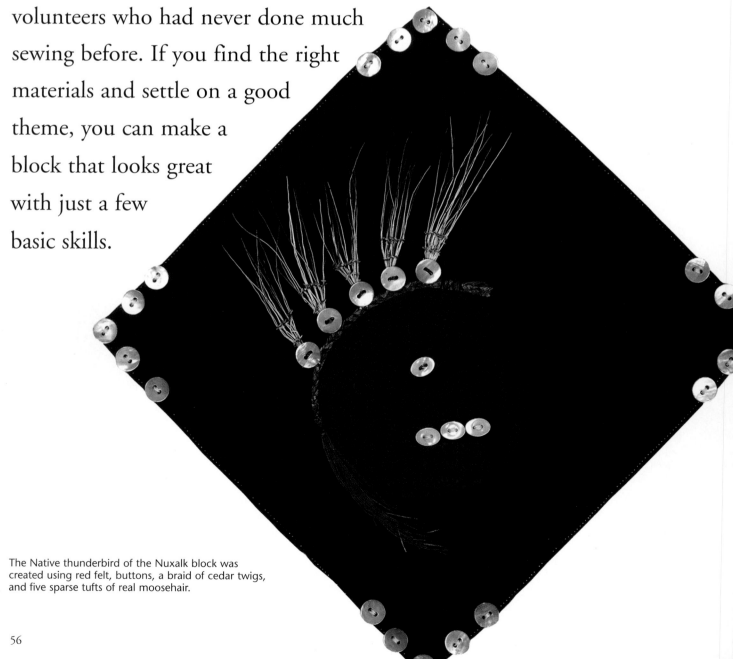

The Native thunderbird of the Nuxalk block was created using red felt, buttons, a braid of cedar twigs, and five sparse tufts of real moosehair.

To get started on your quilt piece, you first have to choose the best items to work with. Some of the Quilt of Belonging's most interesting squares combine traditional fabrics with materials that are so much a part of the culture they represent: the Mi'kmaq square features an eight-pointed Native star made from porcupine quills; a miniature ceremonial dagger hangs in the middle of the block for Yemen; a section of hand-woven lace is the centre-piece of the Belgian block (see The Blocks from A to Z on pages 60–63).

The block for Lesotho — a shepherd tending his modest flock — was made from pieces of a traditional African cotton fabric called *seshoeshoe*.

For your own block, try to think of items that will help tell the story you want to relate. Of course, you don't need to restrict yourself to your family history, the way the block-makers for the Quilt of Belonging did. Your block can be about whatever you want. You may want to say something about the town you live in, the school you go to, the friends you hang out with, or the sports you enjoy — anything that will tell people a bit about who you are.

Let's say you're a baseball fanatic, for example, and you want to make a quilt square that celebrates your love of the game. Why not try peeling the leather off an old ball and working that into your block, along with some fabric in the colours of your favourite team? Anything you can think of is fair to use. You can decorate your block with leaves and flowers from your garden, pictures of you and your friends, ticket stubs from concerts or movies you loved, or stories you cut out from the school newspaper.

No need for a needle and thread! There are plenty of no-sew options that will work just as well. If you

A handmade doll called a *kotomisi* smiles out from the block for Suriname, a former Dutch slave colony on the northeast coast of South America.

The embroidered clock face of the Switzerland block looked more authentic when the makers added two real clock hands.

want to make a music-themed block, for instance, you can simply glue pieces of sheet music or covers from your favourite CDs to a cardboard backing. And how about using an old guitar string as a border?

Creating a virtual quilt block on your computer is another option. It's pretty easy to draw out a square and then fill it in with copyright-free images you download from the Internet. Some graphics programs even have simple templates you may be able to use to get started. Once you're feeling more confident, you can experiment with adding textures and colours and special effects. If you have access to a good-quality colour printer, you can print out the finished product. Or just leave it on your hard drive and use it as a screen saver.

If you're feeling really ambitious, gather all your schoolmates and have each of them contribute a block to a classroom-wide quilt of belonging. You can even organize an old-fashioned quilting bee to put the finished blocks together. You may be surprised by all the things you learn about your friends when you see the pieces they make!

The square for Panama — a wild-looking fish with its skeleton exposed — was made using *mola*, the signature craft of one of the country's Native tribes.

The Blocks from A to Z

We didn't have room to show all 263 blocks, but here's a list of every nation that's included in the actual Quilt of Belonging. You can visit the quilt's website at www.invitationproject.ca. The online gallery has pictures of each individual block, along with information about the way it was made and the place it represents. Better still, see the quilt itself when it comes to your town or a community nearby.

Abenaki
Afghanistan
Albania
Algeria
Algonquin
Andorra
Angola
Antigua and
    Barbuda
Argentina
Armenia
Atikamekw
Australia
Austria
Azerbaijan

Bahamas
Bahrain
Bangladesh
Barbados
Beaver
Belarus
Belgium

Belize
Benin
Beothuk
Bhutan
Blackfoot
Bolivia
Bosnia-Herzegovina
Botswana
Brazil
Brunei
Bulgaria
Burkina Faso
Burma
Burundi

Cambodia
Cameroon
Canada
Cape Verde
Carrier
Cayuga
Central African
    Republic
Chad
Chile
China
Chipewyan
Colombia
Comoros
Congo, Democratic
    Republic of
    Congo
    (Brazzaville)
Costa Rica
Côte d'Ivoire
Cree, Central
Cree, East
Cree, Plains

Croatia
Cuba
Cyprus
Czech
    Republic

Dakota
Denmark
Djibouti
Dogrib
Dominica
Dominican Republic

Ecuador
Egypt
El Salvador
England
Equatorial Guinea
Eritrea
Estonia
Ethiopia

Fiji
Finland
France

Gabon
Gambia
Georgia
Germany
Ghana
Gibraltar
Gitksan
Greece
Grenada
Guatemala
Guinea
Guinea-Bissau
Guyana
Gwich'in

Haida
Haisla
Haiti
Hare
Heiltsuk
Honduras
Hungary

Iceland
India
Indonesia
Inuvialuit
Iran
Iraq
Ireland
Israel
Italy

Jamaica
Japan
Jordan

Kainai (Blood)
Kanien'Kehaka
    (Mohawk)
Kaska
Kazakhstan
Kenya
Kiribati
Kitikmeot (Inuit)
Kivalliq (Inuit)
Korea
Ktunaxa
Kuwait
Kwakwaka'wakw
    (Kwakiutl)
Kyrgyzstan

Labrador (Inuit)
Lakota (Sioux)
(continued)

61

Laos
Latvia
Lebanon
Leni'Lenape
   (Delaware)
Lesotho
Liberia
Libya
Liechtenstein
Lillooet
Lithuania
Luxembourg

Macedonia
Madagascar
Malawai
Malaysia
Maldives
Mali
Maliseet
Malta
Mauritania
Mauritius
Métis
Mexico
Mi'kmaq
Moldova
Monaco
Mongolia
Montagnais (Innu)
Morocco
Mozambique

Nakoda
Namibia
Naskapi
Nauru
Nepal
Netherlands
New Zealand
Nicaragua

Niger
Nigeria
Nisga'a
Nootka
Northern
   Ireland
Norway
Nunavik (Inuit)
Nuxalk

Odawa
Ojibwe
Okanagan
Oman
Oneida
Onondaga
Oweekeno

Pakistan
Palestine
Panama
Papua New Guinea
Paraguay
Passamaquoddy
Peigan
Peru
Philippines
Poland
Portugal
Potawatomi

Qatar
Qikiqtani (Inuit)

Romania
Russia
Rwanda

St. Kitts and
   Nevis
St. Lucia

St. Vincent and the
    Grenadines
Salish, Coast
Samoa
San Marino
São Tomé
    e Príncipe
Saudi Arabia
Scotland
Sekani
Seneca
Senegal
Serbia and
    Montenegro
Seychelles
Shuswap
Sierra Leone
Singapore
Slovakia
Slovenia
Solomon Islands
Somalia
Songhee
South Africa
South Slavey
Spain
Sri Lanka
Sudan
Suriname
Swaziland
Sweden
Switzerland
Syria

Tagish
Tahltan
Taiwan
Tajikistan
Tanzania
Thailand
Thompson

Tlingit
Togo
Tonga
Trinidad and
    Tobago
Tsilhqot'in
    (Chilcotin)
Tsimshian
Tsuu T'ina (Sarcee)
Tunisia
Turkey
Turkmenistan
Tuscarora
Tutchone
Tuvalu

Uganda
Ukraine
United Arab
    Emirates
United Kingdom and
    Dependencies
United States of
    America
Uruguay
Uzbekistan

Vanuatu
Venezuela
Vietnam

Wales
Wendat

Yellowknife
Yemen

Zambia
Zimbabwe

Index